16. JUL 1989

2 5 NOV 2005

198

THE KINGFISHER

AMY CLAMPITT

The Kingfisher

ff

faber and faber

LONDON · BOSTON

First published in the United States of America in 1983
by Alfred A. Knopf, Inc., New York
and simultaneously in Canada
by Random House of Canada Limited, Toronto
First published in Great Britain in 1984
by Faber and Faber Limited
3 Queen Square London WC1N 3AU
Printed in Great Britain by
Whitstable Litho Limited
Whitstable Kent
All rights reserved

British Library Cataloguing in Publication Data

Clampitt, Amy
The kingfisher
I. Title
811'.54   PS3553,L23

ISBN 0-571-13269-3

For Hal

As kingfishers catch fire, dragonflies draw flame . . .

Gerard Manley Hopkins

CONTENTS

ACKNOWLEDGEMENTS

For their help with this book, the author wishes to record her thanks to Mary Jo Salter, Doris Myers, Linda Spencer, John Macrae III, Howard Moss, Frederick Turner, Brad Leithauser, Ann Close, Alice Quinn, and Harold Korn.

Grateful acknowledgement is made to the following periodicals, in which poems in this collection have previously appeared: the *Atlantic Monthly:* Fog", "On the Disadvantages of Central Heating", "Slow Motion"; *Chicago Review:* "Gradual Clearing"; the *Christian Science Monitor:* "The Edge of the Hurricane", "Trasimene" (under the title "Umbrian Painters"); the *Kenyon Review:* "Imago", "Rain at Bellagio"; the *Nation:* "The Outer Bar"; *New England Review:* "A Procession at Candlemas"; the *New Republic:* "Beach Glass", "Marine Surface, Low Overcast"; the *New Yorker:* "Beethoven Opus 111", "Camouflage", "The Cove", "The Kingfisher", "Lindenbloom", "The Quarry", "Salvage", "The Smaller Orchid" (under the title "Ladies' Tresses"), "The Sun Underfoot Among the Sundews", "Tepoztlán"; *Poetry:* "Balms"; *Poetry Northwest:* "Sunday Music"; *Prairie Schooner:* "Botanical Nomenclature", "Meridian", "A Resumption, or Possibly a Remission", "The Woodlot"; and the *Yale Review:* "Stacking the Straw".

THE COVE

Inside the snug house, blue willow-ware
plates go round the dado, cross-stitch
domesticates the guest room, whole nutmegs
inhabit the spice rack, and when there's fog
or a gale we get a fire going, listen
to Mozart, read Marianne Moore, or
sit looking out at the eiders, trig
in their white-over-black as they tip
and tuck themselves into the swell, almost
as though diving under the eiderdown
in a *gemütlich* hotel room at Innsbruck.

At dusk we watch a porcupine, hoary
quadruped, emerge from under the spruce trees,
needle-tined paddle tail held out straight
behind, as though the ground were negotiable
only by climbing, to examine the premises,
and then withdraw from the (we presume)
alarming realm of the horizontal into
the up-and-down underbrush of normality.

From the sundeck, overhung by a gale-
hugged mountain ash, limbs blotched
and tufted with lichen, where in good
weather, every time we look up there's
a new kind of warbler flirting, all ombré
and fine stitchery, through the foliage,
one midday, looking down at the grass
we noticed a turtle—domed repoussé

leather with an underlip of crimson—
as it hove eastward, a covered
wagon intent on the wrong direction.

Where at low tide the rocks, like the
back of an old sheepdog or spaniel, are
rugg'd with wet seaweed, the cove
embays a pavement of ocean, at times
wrinkling like tinfoil, at others
all isinglass flakes, or sun-pounded
gritty glitter of mica; or hanging
intact, a curtain wall just frescoed
indigo, so immense a hue, a blue
of such majesty it can't be looked at,
at whose apex there pulses, even
in daylight, a lighthouse, light-
pierced like a needle's eye.

FOG

A vagueness comes over everything,
as though proving color and contour
alike dispensable: the lighthouse
extinct, the islands' spruce-tips
drunk up like milk in the
universal emulsion; houses
reverting into the lost
and forgotten; granite
subsumed, a rumor
in a mumble of ocean.
                              Tactile
definition, however, has not been
totally banished: hanging
tassel by tassel, panicled
foxtail and needlegrass,
dropseed, furred hawkweed,
and last season's rose-hips
are vested in silenced
chimes of the finest,
clearest sea-crystal.
                              Opacity
opens up rooms, a showcase
for the hueless moonflower
corolla, as Georgia
O'Keeffe might have seen it,
of foghorns; the nodding
campanula of bell buoys;
the ticking, linear
filigree of bird voices.   17

GRADUAL CLEARING

Late in the day the fog
wrung itself out like a sponge
in glades of rain,
sieving the half-invisible
cove with speartips;
then, in a lifting
of wisps and scarves, of smoke-rings
from about the islands, disclosing
what had been wavering
fishnet plissé as a smoothness
of peau-de-soie or just-ironed
percale, with a tatting
of foam out where the rocks are,
the sheened no-color of it,
the bandings of platinum
and magnesium suffusing,
minute by minute, with clandestine
rose and violet, with opaline
nuance of milkweed, a texture
not to be spoken of above a whisper,
began, all along the horizon,
gradually to unseal
like the lip of a cave
or of a cavernous,
single, pearl-
engendering seashell.

THE OUTER BAR

When through some lacuna, chink, or interstice
in the unlicensed free-for-all that goes
on without a halt out there all day, all night,
all through the winter,

one morning at low tide you walk dry-shod across
a shadow isthmus to the outer bar,
you find yourself, once over, sinking at every step
into a luscious mess—

a vegetation of unbarbered, virgin, foot-thick
velvet, the air you breathe an aromatic
thicket, odors in confusion starting up
at every step like partridges

or schools of fishes, an element you swim through
as to an unplanned, headily illicit
interview. The light out there, gashed
by the surf's scimitar,

is blinding, a rebuke—Go back! Go back!—
behind the silhouetted shipwreck (Whose?
When did it happen? Back in the village
nobody can tell you),

the bell buoy hunkering knee-deep in foam,
a blood-red-painted harbinger. How strange
a rim, back where you came from,
of familiar portents

reviewed from this *isola bella,* paradise
inside a prison rockpile—the unravished
protégé of guardians so lawless, refuge
moated up in such a shambles!

Your mind keeps turning back to look at them—
chain-gang archangels that in their prismatic
frenzy fall, gall and gash the daylight
out there, all through the winter.

SEA MOUSE

The orphanage of possibility
has had to be expanded to
admit the sea mouse. No one
had asked for such a thing,
or prophesied its advent,

sheltering under ruching
edges of sea lettuce—
a wet thing but pettable
as, seen in the distance,
the tops of copses,

sun-honeyed, needle-pelted
pine trees, bearded barley,
or anything newborn not bald
but furred. No rodent this
scabrous, this unlooked-for

foundling, no catnip plaything
for a cat to worry, not even
an echinoderm, the creature
seems to be a worm. Silk-spiny,
baby-mummy-swaddled, it's

at home where every corridor
is mop-and-bucket scrubbed
and aired from wall to wall
twice daily by the inde-
fatigable tidal head nurse.

BEACH GLASS

While you walk the water's edge,
turning over concepts
I can't envision, the honking buoy
serves notice that at any time
the wind may change,
the reef-bell clatters
its treble monotone, deaf as Cassandra
to any note but warning. The ocean,
cumbered by no business more urgent
than keeping open old accounts
that never balanced,
goes on shuffling its millenniums
of quartz, granite, and basalt.
                              It behaves
toward the permutations of novelty—
driftwood and shipwreck, last night's
beer cans, spilt oil, the coughed-up
residue of plastic—with random
impartiality, playing catch or tag
or touch-last like a terrier,
turning the same thing over and over,
over and over. For the ocean, nothing
is beneath consideration.
                              The houses
of so many mussels and periwinkles
have been abandoned here, it's hopeless
to know which to salvage. Instead
I keep a lookout for beach glass—
amber of Budweiser, chrysoprase

of Almadén and Gallo, lapis
by way of (no getting around it,
I'm afraid) Phillips'
Milk of Magnesia, with now and then a rare
translucent turquoise or blurred amethyst
of no known origin.
                    The process
goes on forever: they came from sand,
they go back to gravel,
along with the treasuries
of Murano, the buttressed
astonishments of Chartres,
which even now are readying
for being turned over and over as gravely
and gradually as an intellect
engaged in the hazardous
redefinition of structures
no one has yet looked at.

MARINE SURFACE,
LOW OVERCAST

Out of churned aureoles
this buttermilk, this
herringbone of albatross,
floss of mercury,
déshabille of spun
aluminum, furred with a velouté
of looking-glass,

a stuff so single
it might almost be lifted,
folded over, crawled underneath
or slid between, as nakedness-
caressing sheets, or donned
and worn, the train-borne
trapping of an unrepeatable
occasion,

this wind-silver
rumpling as of oatfields,
a suede of meadow,
a nub, a nap, a mane of lustre
lithe as the slide
of muscle in its
sheath of skin,

laminae of living tissue,
mysteries of flex,
affinities of texture,
subtleties of touch, of pressure

and release, the suppleness
of long and intimate
association,

new synchronies of fingertip,
of breath, of sequence,
entities that still can rouse,
can stir or solder,
whip to a froth, or force
to march in strictly
hierarchical formation

down galleries of sheen, of flux,
cathedral domes that seem to hover
overturned and shaken like a basin
to the noise of voices,
from a rustle to the jostle
of such rush-hour
conglomerations

no loom, no spinneret, no forge, no factor,
no process whatsoever, patent
applied or not applied for,
no five-year formula, no fabric
for which pure imagining,
except thus prompted,
can invent the equal.

THE SUN UNDERFOOT
AMONG THE SUNDEWS

An ingenuity too astonishing
to be quite fortuitous is
this bog full of sundews, sphagnum-
lined and shaped like a teacup.
                                    A step
down and you're into it; a
wilderness swallows you up:
ankle-, then knee-, then midriff-
to-shoulder-deep in wetfooted
understory, an overhead
spruce-tamarack horizon hinting
you'll never get out of here.
                                    But the sun
among the sundews, down there,
is so bright, an underfoot
webwork of carnivorous rubies,
a star-swarm thick as the gnats
they're set to catch, delectable
double-faced cockleburs, each
hair-tip a sticky mirror
afire with sunlight, a million
of them and again a million,
each mirror a trap set to
unhand unbelieving,

                    that either
a First Cause said once, "Let there
be sundews," and there were, or they've
made their way here unaided
other than by that backhand, round-
about refusal to assume responsibility
known as Natural Selection.
                              But the sun
underfoot is so dazzling
down there among the sundews,
there is so much light
in the cup that, looking,
you start to fall upward.

BOTANICAL
NOMENCLATURE

Down East people, not being botanists,
call it "that pink-and-blue flower
you find along the shore." Wildflower
guides, their minds elsewhere, mumble
"sea lungwort or oysterleaf" as a label
for these recumbent roundels, foliage
blued to a driftwood patina
growing outward, sometimes to the
size of a cathedral window,
stemrib grisaille edge-tasseled
with opening goblets, with bugles
in miniature, mauve through cerulean,
toggled into a seawall scree,
these tuffets of skyweed
neighbored by a climbing tideline,
by the holdfasts, the gargantuan lariats
of kelp, a landfall of seaweed:

Mertensia, the learned Latin
handle, proving the uses of taxonomy,
shifts everything abruptly inland,
childhoodward, to what we called then
(though not properly) bluebells:
spring-bottomland glades standing upright,
their lake-evoking sky color
a trapdoor, a window letting in distances
all the way to the ocean—
reaching out, *nolens volens,*
as one day everything breathing

will reach out, with just such
bells on its fingers, to touch
without yet quite having seen
the unlikelihood, the ramifying
happenstance, the mirroring
marryings of all likeness.

ON THE DISADVANTAGES
OF CENTRAL HEATING

cold nights on the farm, a sock-shod
stove-warmed flatiron slid under
the covers, mornings a damascene-
sealed bizarrerie of fernwork
      decades ago now

waking in northwest London, tea
brought up steaming, a Peak Frean
biscuit alongside to be nibbled
as blue gas leaps up singing
      decades ago now

damp sheets in Dorset, fog-hung
habitat of bronchitis, of long
hot soaks in the bathtub, of nothing
quite drying out till next summer:
      delicious to think of

hassocks pulled in close, toasting-
forks held to coal-glow, strong-minded
small boys and big eager sheepdogs
muscling in on bookish profundities
      now quite forgotten

the farmhouse long sold, old friends
dead or lost track of, what's salvaged
is this vivid diminuendo, unfogged
by mere affect, the perishing residue
      of pure sensation

MERIDIAN

First daylight on the bittersweet-hung
sleeping porch at high summer : dew
all over the lawn, sowing diamond-
point-highlighted shadows :
the hired man's shadow revolving
along the walk, a flash of milkpails
passing : no threat in sight, no hint
anywhere in the universe, of that

apathy at the meridian, the noon
of absolute boredom : flies
crooning black lullabies in the kitchen,
milk-soured crocks, cream separator
still unwashed : what is there to life
but chores and more chores, dishwater,
fatigue, unwanted children : nothing
to stir the longueur of afternoon

except possibly thunderheads :
climbing, livid, turreted alabaster
lit up from within by splendor and terror
—forked lightning's
                split-second disaster.

A RESUMPTION,
OR POSSIBLY A REMISSION

for my sister Beth

Waking to all that white, as week by week
the inland ravines of a two-river city
filled up with it, was like the resumption
of a state of grace, as in dreams of being carried.
Nothing disturbed it: not the owl that came
rowing out at noon, soundless as fur,
nor the great horned ones' profundo
yelp from some outpost among oaks'
dun, nattering cling-leaves. In that
white habitat, the precarious architect
of ledges and cornices, of bridges
suspended with the ease of hammocks, even
those halloos came through as friendly.

Though on days of thaw a ponderous
icicle-fall, a more and more massively
glistening overhang, gave birth to daggers,
and though we'd hear our alcoholic landlord
(he came once beseeching the loan of
a bottle opener) being yelled at
by the spouse-in-charge, who would then
address herself to a parlor organ,
pumping out consolation with a vengeance,
from January nearly to the willowy
landfall of April, when new excitements
and misgivings began to intervene, to live
moated and immured inside the castle-keep
of all that white was to discover
even the Ur-nightmare of being

dropped, of waking up abandoned,
gone miraculously into remission.

I find I can no longer summon the layout
of that apartment. But the scene outside it
either reinvents, or subsumes uninterrupted,
a state that can't be gone back to: from
one window a pair of cardinals, she olive-
muted and red of beak, as though (you said)
she'd put on lipstick, he the scarlet-
suited royal mite of a Goya portrait,
meteors' scathing anomaly slowed down
and mollified to a quasi-domestic,
seed-eating familiar; next door
a silent house, walks uncleared week
after week, snowdrifts accumulating,
their tented pavilions overhung
by an old, crone-dark catalpa
metamorphosing, snowfall by snowfall,
into a hammock, the burden of all
that white, the deepening sag of it,
upheld as by a nursing mother.

A PROCESSION AT CANDLEMAS

Moving on or going back to where you came from,
bad news is what you mainly travel with:
a breakup or a breakdown, someone running off

or walking out, called up or called home:
death in the family. Nudged from their stanchions
outside the terminal, anonymous of purpose

as a flock of birds, the bison of the highway
funnel westward onto Route 80, mirroring
an entity that cannot look into itself and know

what makes it what it is. Sooner or later
every trek becomes a funeral procession.
The mother curtained in Intensive Care—

a scene the mind leaves blank, fleeing instead
toward scenes of transhumance, the belled sheep
moving up the Pyrenees, red-tasseled pack llamas

footing velvet-green precipices, the Kurdish
women, jingling with bangles, gorgeous
on their rug-piled mounts—already lying dead,

bereavement altering the moving lights
to a processional, a feast of Candlemas.
Change as child-bearing, birth as a kind

of shucking off: out of what began
as a Mosaic insult—such a loathing
of the common origin, even a virgin,

having given birth, needs purifying—
to carry fire as though it were a flower,
the terror and the loveliness entrusted

into naked hands, supposing God might have,
might actually need a mother: people have
at times found this a way of being happy.

A Candlemas of moving lights along Route 80;
lighted candles in a corridor from Arlington
over the Potomac, for every carried flame

the name of a dead soldier: an element
fragile as ego, frightening as parturition,
necessary and intractable as dreaming.

The lapped, wheelborne integument, layer
within layer, at the core a dream of
something precious, ripped: Where are we?

The sleepers groan, stir, rewrap themselves
about the self's imponderable substance,
or clamber down, numb-footed, half in a drowse

of freezing dark, through a Stonehenge
of fuel pumps, the bison hulks slantwise
beside them, drinking. What is real except

what's fabricated? The jellies glitter
cream-capped in the cafeteria showcase;
gumball globes, Life Savers cinctured

in parcel gilt, plop from their housings
perfect, like miracles. Comb, nail clipper,
lip rouge, mirrors and emollients embody,

niched into the washroom wall case,
the pristine seductiveness of money.
Absently, without inhabitants, this

nowhere oasis wears the place name
of Indian Meadows. The westward-trekking
transhumance, once only, of a people who,

in losing everything they had, lost even
the names they went by, stumbling past
like caribou, perhaps camped here. Who

can assign a trade-in value to that sorrow?
The monk in sheepskin over tucked-up saffron
intoning to a drum becomes the metronome

of one more straggle up Pennsylvania Avenue
in falling snow, a whirl of tenderly
remorseless corpuscles, street gangs

amok among magnolias' pregnant wands,
a stillness at the heart of so much whirling:
beyond the torn integument of childbirth,

sometimes, wrapped like a papoose into a grief
not merely of the ego, you rediscover almost
the rest-in-peace of the placental coracle.

2

Of what the dead were, living, one knows
so little as barely to recognize
the fabric of the backward-ramifying

antecedents, half-noted presences
in darkened rooms: the old, the feared,
the hallowed. Never the same river

drowns the unalterable doorsill. An effigy
in olive wood or pear wood, dank
with the sweat of age, walled in the dark

at Brauron, Argos, Samos: even the unwed
Athene, who had no mother, born—it's declared—
of some man's brain like every other pure idea,

had her own wizened cult object, kept
out of sight like the incontinent whimperer
in the backstairs bedroom, where no child

ever goes—to whom, year after year,
the fair linen of the sacred peplos
was brought in ceremonial procession—

flutes and stringed instruments, wildflower-
hung cattle, nubile Athenian girls, young men
praised for the beauty of their bodies. Who

can unpeel the layers of that seasonal
returning to the dark where memory fails,
as birds re-enter the ancestral flyway?

Daylight, snow falling, knotting of gears:
Chicago. Soot, the rotting backsides
of tenements, grimed trollshapes of ice

underneath the bridges, the tunnel heaving
like a birth canal. Disgorged, the infant
howling in the restroom; steam-table cereal,

pale coffee; wall-eyed TV receivers, armchairs
of molded plastic: the squalor of the day
resumed, the orphaned litter taken up again

unloved, the spawn of botched intentions,
grief a mere hardening of the gut,
a set piece of what can't be avoided:

parents by the tens of thousands living
unthanked, unpaid but in the sour coin
of resentment. Midmorning gray as zinc

along Route 80, corn-stubble quilting
the underside of snowdrifts, the cadaverous
belvedere of windmills, the sullen stare

of feedlot cattle; black creeks puncturing
white terrain, the frozen bottomland
a mush of willow tops; dragnetted in ice,

the Mississippi. Westward toward the dark,
the undertow of scenes come back to, fright
riddling the structures of interior history:

Where is it? Where, in the shucked-off
bundle, the hampered obscurity that has been
for centuries the mumbling lot of women,

did the thread of fire, too frail
ever to discover what it meant, to risk
even the taking of a shape, relinquish

the seed of possibility, unguessed-at
as a dream of something precious? Memory,
that exquisite blunderer, stumbling

like a migrant bird that finds the flyway
it hardly knew it knew except by instinct,
down the long-unentered nave of childhood,

late on a midwinter afternoon, alone
among the snow-hung hollows of the windbreak
on the far side of the orchard, encounters

sheltering among the evergreens, a small
stilled bird, its cap of clear yellow
slit by a thread of scarlet—the untouched

nucleus of fire, the lost connection
hallowing the wizened effigy, the mother
curtained in Intensive Care: a Candlemas

of moving lights along Route 80, at nightfall,
in falling snow, the stillness and the sorrow
40 of things moving back to where they came from.

THE EDGE
OF THE HURRICANE

Wheeling, the careening
winds arrive with lariats
and tambourines of rain.
Torn-to-pieces, mud-dark
flounces of Caribbean

cumulus keep passing,
keep passing.   By afternoon
rinsed transparencies begin
to open overhead, Mediterranean
windowpanes of clearness

crossed by young gusts'
vaporous fripperies, liquid
footprints flying, lacewing
leaf-shade brightening
and fading. Sibling

gales stand up on point
in twirling fouettés
of debris. The day ends
bright, cloud-wardrobe
packed away. Nightfall

hangs up a single moon
bleached white as laundry,
serving notice yet again how
levity can also trample,
drench, wring and mangle.

SALVAGE

Daily the cortege of crumpled
defunct cars
goes by by the lasagna-
layered flatbed
truckload: hardtop

reverting to tar smudge,
wax shine antiqued to crusted
winepress smear,
windshield battered to
intact ice-tint, a rarity

fresh from the Pleistocene.
I like it; privately
I find esthetic
satisfaction in these
ceremonial removals

from the category of
received ideas
to regions where pigeons'
svelte smoke-velvet
limousines, taxiing

in whirligigs, reclaim
a parking lot,
and the bag-laden
hermit woman, disencumbered
of a greater incubus,

the crush of unexamined
attitudes, stoutly
follows her routine,
mining the mountainsides
of our daily refuse

for artifacts: subversive
re-establishing
with each arcane
trash-basket dig
the pleasures of the ruined.

BALMS

Hemmed in by the prim
deodorizing stare
of the rare-book room,
I stumbled over,
lodged under glass, a
revenant *Essay on Color*
by Mary Gartside, a woman
I'd never heard of, open
to a hand-rendered
watercolor illustration
wet-bright as the day
its unadulterated red-
and-yellow was laid on
(publication date 1818).

Garden nasturtium hues,
the text alongside
explained, had been
her guide. Sudden as
on hands and knees
I felt the smell of them
suffuse the catacomb
so much of us lives in—
horned, pungent, velvet-
eared succulence, a perfume
without hokum, the intimate
of trudging earthworms
and everyone's last end's
unnumbered, milling tenants.

Most olfactory experience
either rubs your nose
in it or tries to flatter
with a funeral home's
approximation of such balms
as a theology of wax alone
can promise, and the bees
deliver. Mary Gartside
died, I couldn't even
learn the year. Our one
encounter occurred by chance
where pure hue set loose
unearthly gusts of odor
from earthbound nasturtiums.

LINDENBLOOM

Before midsummer density
opaques with shade the checker-
tables underneath, in daylight
unleafing lindens burn
green-gold a day or two,
no more, with intimations
of an essence I saw once,
in what had been the pleasure-
garden of the popes
at Avignon, dishevel

into half (or possibly three-
quarters of) a million
hanging, intricately
tactile, blond bell-pulls
of bloom, the in-mid-air
resort of honeybees'
hirsute cotillion
teasing by the milligram
out of those necklaced
nectaries, aromas

so intensely subtle,
strollers passing under
looked up confused,
as though they'd just
heard voices, or
inhaled the ghost
of derelict splendor
and/or of seraphs shaken
into pollen dust
no transubstantiating
pope or antipope could sift
or quite precisely ponder.

CAMOUFLAGE

for Jo and Roy Shaw

It seemed at first like a piece of luck,
the discovery, there in the driveway,
of an odd sort of four-leaf clover—
no bankful of three-penny greenery
but a worried, hovering, wing-dragging
      killdeer's treasury—

a mosaic of four lopsided olives
or marbles you had to hunt
to find again every time, set into
the gravel as if by accident.
We'd have turned that bird's
      entire environment

upside down to have preserved them.
But what was there, after all,
we could have told her about foxes,
coons, cats, or the vandal
with its eye out for whatever anyone
      considers special?

In her bones, in her genes, in
the secret code of her behavior,
she already knew more than all our
bumbling daydreams, our palaver
about safeguards, could muster
      the wit to decipher:

how her whereabouts could vanish
into the gravel, how that brilliant
double-looped necklace could amputate
into invisibility the chevroned
cinnamon of her plumage. Cleverer
       than any mere learned,

merely devious equivocation,
that broken-wing pageant—
who taught her that? We have
no answer except accident,
the trillion-times-over-again
       repeated predicament

sifted with so spendthrift
a disregard for casualties
we can hardly bear to think of
a system so heartless, so shiftless
as being in charge here. It's
       too much like us—

except, after having looked so close
and so long at that casual handful
of dice, squiggle-spotted by luck
that made them half invisible,
watching too often the waltzing swoop
       of the bird's arrival

had meant a disruption of more usual
habits. For all our reading in the papers
about blunderers and risk-takers with
the shrug of nothing-much-matters-
how-those-things-turn-out, we'd unlearned
      to be good losers.

Sorrow, so far as we know, is not
part of a shorebird's equipment.
Nor is memory, of either survival
or losing, after the event.
Having squandered our attention, we
      were less prudent.

For a day, we couldn't quite afford
that morning's black discovery.
Grief is like money: there is only
so much of it we can give away.
And that much grief, for a day,
      bankrupted our economy.

THE KINGFISHER

In a year the nightingales were said to be so loud
they drowned out slumber, and peafowl strolled screaming
beside the ruined nunnery, through the long evening
of a dazzled pub crawl, the halcyon color, portholed
by those eye-spots' stunning tapestry, unsettled
the pastoral nightfall with amazements opening.

Months later, intermission in a pub on Fifty-fifth Street
found one of them still breathless, the other quizzical,
acting the philistine, puncturing Stravinsky—"Tell
me, what *was* that racket in the orchestra about?"—
hauling down the Firebird, harum-scarum, like a kite,
a burnished, breathing wreck that didn't hurt at all.

Among the Bronx Zoo's exiled jungle fowl, they heard
through headphones of a separating panic, the bellbird
reiterate its single *chong,* a scream nobody answered.
When he mourned, "The poetry is gone," she quailed,
seeing how his hands shook, sobered into feeling old.
By midnight, yet another fifth would have been killed.

A Sunday morning, the November of their cataclysm
(Dylan Thomas brought in *in extremis* to St. Vincent's,
that same week, a symptomatic datum) found them
wandering a downtown churchyard. Among its headstones,
while from unruined choirs the noise of Christendom
poured over Wall Street, a benison in vestments,

a late thrush paused, in transit from some grizzled
spruce bog to the humid equatorial fireside: berry-
eyed, bark-brown above, with dark hints of trauma
in the stigmata of its underparts—or so, too bruised
just then to have invented anything so fancy,
later, re-embroidering a retrospect, she had supposed.

In gray England, years of muted recrimination (then
dead silence) later, she could not have said how many
spoiled takeoffs, how many entanglements gone sodden,
how many gaudy evenings made frantic by just one
insomniac nightingale, how many liaisons gone down
screaming in a stroll beside the ruined nunnery;

a kingfisher's burnished plunge, the color
of felicity afire, came glancing like an arrow
through landscapes of untended memory: ardor
illuminating with its terrifying currency
now no mere glimpse, no porthole vista
but, down on down, the uninhabitable sorrow.

THE SMALLER ORCHID

Love is a climate
small things find safe
to grow in—not
(though I once supposed so)
the demanding cattleya
du côté de chez Swann,
glamor among the faubourgs,
hothouse overpowerings, blisses
and cruelties at teatime, but this
next-to-unidentifiable wildling,
hardly more than a
sprout, I've found
flourishing in the hollows
of a granite seashore—
a cheerful tousle, little,
white, down-to-earth orchid
declaring its authenticity,
if you hug the ground
close enough, in a powerful
outdoorsy-domestic
whiff of vanilla.

A HAIRLINE FRACTURE

Whatever went wrong, that week, was more than weather:
a shoddy streak in the fabric of the air of London
that disintegrated into pollen
and came charging down by the bushelful,
an abrasive the color of gold dust, eroding
the tearducts and littering the sidewalks
in the neighborhood of Sloane Square,

where the Underground's upper reaches have the character,
almost, of a Roman ruin—from one
crannied arcade a dustmop of yellow blossom
hung with the stubborn insolence of the unintended,
shaking still other mischief from its hair
onto the platform, the pneumatic haste of missed
trains, the closing barrier—

wherever we went, between fits of sneezing we quarreled:
under the pallid entablatures of Belgravia,
the busy brown façades that were all angles
going in and out like a bellows, even the small house
on Ebury Street where Mozart, at the age of eight,
wrote his first symphony, our difference
was not to be composed.

Unmollified by the freckled plush of mushrooming
monkeyflowers in the windowboxes of Chelsea, undone
by the miraculous rift in the look of things
when you've just arrived—the remote up close,
the knowing that in another, unentered existence
everything shimmering at the surface is this minute
merely, unremarkably familiar—

it was as though we watched the hairline fracture
of the quotidian widen to a geomorphic fissure,
its canyon edge bridged by the rainbows of a terror
that nothing would ever again be right
between us, that wherever we went, nowhere
in the universe would the bone again be knit
or the rift be closed.

SLOW MOTION

Her liquid look as dark
as antique honey,
the auburn of her hide
improbably domestic,
the color of a collie or a
Jersey calf, she occupied
(unantlered, a knob-jointed
monument to mild inquiry)

the total sun of that July
mid-morning. Astonishment
sometimes (as it moved
then) moves slowly
to fill up the heart's abruptly
enormous hollow
with stilled cold
as from a well.

Daring her, I stole
a step. One ear
shifted its ponderous
velour to winnow
what my own bare
tympanum merely spilled
and scattered like
a gust of lost pollen.

The meshes of a life
at close attention
went dense; the heaved
limbs upended slowly,
the white scut half-
lifted in a lopsided
wigwag, as though
even the wildest of
surmises need be
in no great hurry.

SUNDAY MUSIC

The Baroque sewing machine of Georg Friedrich
going back, going back to stitch back together
scraps of a scheme that's outmoded, all
those lopsidedly overblown expectations
now severely in need of revision, re
the nature of things, or more precisely
(back a stitch, back a stitch) the
nature of going forward.

No longer footpath-perpendicular, a monody
tootled on antelope bone, no longer
wheelbarrow heave-ho, the nature of going
forward is not perspective, not stairways,
not, as for the muse of Josquin or Gesualdo,
sostenuto, a leaning together
in memory of, things held onto
fusing and converging,

nor is it any longer an orbit, tonality's
fox-and-goose footprints going round
and round in the snow, the centripetal
force of the dominant. The nature of next
is not what we seem to be hearing
or imagine we feel: is not dance,
is not melody, not elegy,
is not even chemistry,

not Mozart leaching out seraphs
from a sieve of misfortune. The nature
of next is not fugue or rondo, not footpath
or wheelbarrow track, not steamships'
bass vibrations, but less and less
knowing what to expect, it's
the rate of historical
change going faster

and faster: it's noise, it's droids' stone-
deaf intergalactic twitter, it's get ready
to disconnect!—no matter how filled
our heads are with backed-up old
tunes, with polyphony, with basso
profundo fioritura, with this Concerto
Grosso's delectable (back a stitch,
back a stitch) Allegro.

BEETHOVEN, OPUS 111

for Norman Carey

There are epochs . . . when mankind, not con-
tent with the present, longing for time's deeper
layers, like the plowman, thirsts for the virgin
soil of time.

—OSIP MANDELSTAM

—Or, conversely, hungers
for the levitations of the concert hall:
the hands like rafts of *putti*
out of a region where the dolorous stars
are fixed in glassy cerements of Art;
the *ancien régime*'s diaphanous plash
athwart the mounting throb of hobnails—
shod squadrons of vibration
mining the air, its struck ores hardening
into a plowshare, a downward wandering
disrupting every formal symmetry:
from the supine harp-case, the strung-foot
tendons under the mahogany, the bulldozer
in the bass unearths a Piranesian
catacomb: Beethoven ventilating,
with a sound he cannot hear, the cave-in
of recurring rage.
                In the tornado country
of mid-America, my father
might have been his twin—a farmer
hacking at sourdock, at the strangle-
roots of thistles and wild morning glories,
setting out rashly, one October,

to rid the fencerows of poison ivy:
livid seed-globs turreted
in trinities of glitter, ripe
with the malefic glee no farmer doubts
lives deep down things. My father
was naïve enough—by nature
revolutionary, though he'd have
disowned the label—to suppose he might
in some way, minor but radical, disrupt
the givens of existence: set
his neighbors' thinking straight, undo
the stranglehold of reasons nations
send their boys off to war. That fall,
after the oily fireworks had cooled down
to trellises of hairy wicks,
he dug them up, rootstocks and all,
and burned them. Do-gooder!
The well-meant holocaust became
a mist of venom, sowing itself along
the sculptured hollows of his overalls,
braceleting wrists and collarbone—
a mesh of blisters spreading to a shirt
worn like a curse. For weeks
he writhed inside it. Awful.

                              High art
with a stiff neck: an upright Steinway
bought in Chicago; a chromo of a Hobbema
tree-avenue, or of Millet's imagined peasant,
the lark she listens to invisible, perhaps

irrelevant: harpstrings and fripperies of air
congealed into an object nailed against the wall,
its sole ironic function (if it has any)
to demonstrate that one, though he may
grunt and sweat at work, is not a clod.
Beethoven might declare the air
his domicile, the winds kin, the tornado
a kind of second cousin; here,
his labor merely shimmers—a deracinated
album leaf, a bagatelle, the "Moonlight"
rendered with a dying fall (the chords
subside, disintegrate, regroup
in climbing sequences *con brio*); there's
no dwelling on the sweet past here,
there being no past to speak of
other than the setbacks: typhoid
in the wells, half the first settlers
dead of it before a year was out;
diphtheria and scarlet fever
every winter; drought, the Depression,
a mortgage on the mortgage. High art
as a susurrus, the silk and perfume
of unsullied hands. Those hands!—
driving the impressionable wild with anguish
for another life entirely: the Lyceum circuit,
the doomed diving bell of Art.

                              Beethoven

in his workroom: ear trumpet,
conversation book and pencil, candlestick,

broken crockery, the Graf piano
wrecked by repeated efforts to hear himself—
out of a humdrum squalor the levitations,
the shakes and triplets, the *Adagio
molto semplice e cantabile,* the Arietta
a disintegrating surf of blossom
opening along the keyboard, along the fencerows
the astonishment of sweetness. My father,
driving somewhere in Kansas or Colorado,
in dustbowl country, stopped the car
to dig up by the roots a flower
he'd never seen before—a kind
of prickly poppy most likely, its luminousness
wounding the blank plains like desire.
He mentioned in a letter the disappointment
of his having hoped it might transplant—
an episode that brings me near tears,
still, as even his dying does not—
that awful dying, months-long, hunkered,
irascible. From a clod no plowshare
could deliver, a groan for someone
(because he didn't want to look
at anything) to take away the flowers,
a bawling as of slaughterhouses, slogans
of a general uprising: *Freiheit!*
Beethoven, shut up with the four walls
of his deafness, rehearsing the unhearable
semplice e cantabile, somehow reconstituting
the blister shirt of the intolerable

into these shakes and triplets, a hurrying
into flowering along the fencerows: dying,
for my father, came to be like that
finally—in its messages the levitation
of serenity, as though the spirit might
aspire, in its last act,

                    to walk on air.

THE QUARRY

Fishes swam here through the Eocene
too many fathoms up
to think of without suffocation. Light-years
of ooze foreshortened into limestone
swarm with starfish
remoter than the antiquated
pinpoints of astronomy
beneath the stagecoach laboring,
when the thaws came, through mud
up to the hubs. Midsummer's welling bluestem
rose so high the wagons, prairie schooners
under unmasted coifs of canvas,
dragged belly-deep in grass
across the sloughs.
     No roads,
no landmarks to tell where you are,
or who, or whether you will ever find a place
to feel at home in: no alpine
fastness, no tree-profiled pook's hill,
the habitat of magic: only waves
of chlorophyll in motion, the darkened jetsam
of bur oaks, a serpentine of willows
along the hollows—a flux
that waterlogs the mind, draining southeastward
by osmosis to the Mississippi,
where by night the body of De Soto,
ballasted with sand—or was it armor?—
sank into the ooze, nudged by the barbels,
as it decomposed, of giant catfish. Others,

in a terrain as barren
as the dust of bones, kept the corrupt
obsession going: Gold—greed for the metal
most prized because by nature it's
least corruptible. Flushed finally
out of the heartland drainpipe,
the soft parts of De Soto's body filtered
into the capillaries of the delta.   Will
some shard of skull or jawbone, undecomposed,
outlast his name, as the unquarried starfish
outlast the seas that inundated them?

                                       Think back

a little, to what would have been
without this festering of lights at night,
this grid of homesteads, this hardening
lymph of haste foreshortened into highways:
the lilt and ripple of the dark,
birdsong at dusk augmented by frog choirs
already old before the Eocene; the wickiups
now here, now there, edged westward
year by year, hemmed in or undermined,
done in finally by treaties. The year
the first land office in the territory opened,
when there were still no roads
other than wagon tracks, one Lyman Dillon,
starting at Dubuque, drove a plow southwestward
a hundred miles—the longest furrow
ever, straight into the belly of the future,
where the broken loam would soon

be mounted, as on a howdah, by
a marble capitol, the glister
of whose dome still overtops
the frittered sprawl of who we are,
of where we came from,
with its stilted El Dorado.

THE WOODLOT

Clumped murmuring above a sump of loam—
grass-rich, wood-poor—that first the plow,
then the inventor (his name plowed under
somewhere in the Patent Office) of barbed wire,
taught, if not fine manners, how at least to follow
the surveyor's rule, the woodlot nodes of willow,
evergreen or silver maple gave the prairie grid
what little personality it had.
                                        Who could
have learned fine manners where the air,
that rude nomad, still domineered,
without a shape it chose to keep,
oblivious of section lines, in winter
whisking its wolfish spittle to a froth
that turned whole townships into
one white wallow? Barbed wire
kept in the cattle but would not abrade
the hide or draw the blood
of gales hurled gnashing like seawater over fences'
laddered apertures, rigging the landscape
with the perspective of a shipwreck. Land-chained,
the blizzard paused to caterwaul
at every windbreak, a rage the worse
because it was in no way personal.
                                        Against
the involuted tantrums of spring and summer—
sackfuls of ire, the frightful udder
of the dropped mammocumulus
become all mouth, a lamprey

swigging up whole farmsteads, suction
dislodging treetrunks like a rotten tooth—
luck and a cellarhole were all
a prairie dweller had to count on.
                                              Whether
the inventor of barbed wire was lucky
finally in what he found himself
remembering, who knows? Did he
ever, even once, envision
the spread of what he'd done
across a continent: whale-song's
taut dulcimer still thrumming as it strung together
orchard, barnyard, bullpen, feedlot,
windbreak: wire to be clambered over,
crawled through or slid under, shepherded—
the heifers staring—to an enclosure
whose ceiling's silver-maple tops
stir overhead, uneasy, in the interminably
murmuring air? Deep in it, under
appletrees like figures in a ritual, violets
are thick, a blue cellarhole
of pure astonishment.
                          It is
the earliest memory. Before it,
I/you, whatever that conundrum may yet
prove to be, amounts to nothing.

IMAGO

Sometimes, she remembers, a chipped flint
would turn up in a furrow,
pink as a peony (from the iron in it)
or as the flared throat of a seashell:
a nomad's artifact fished from the broth,
half sea half land—hard evidence
of an unfathomed state of mind.

Nomads. The wagon train that camped
and left its name on Mormon Ridge.
The settlers who moved on to California,
bequeathing a laprobe pieced from the hide
of a dead buffalo, the frail sleigh
that sleeps under the haymow, and a headstone
so small it might be playing house,
for the infant daughter, aged two days,
no name, they also left behind.

Half sea half land: the shirker propped
above her book in a farmhouse parlor
lolls with the merfolk who revert to foam,
eyeing at a distance the lit pavilions
that seduced her, their tailed child,
into the palaces of metamorphosis. She pays
now (though they do not know this)
by treading, at every step she takes,
on a parterre of tomahawks.

A thirst for something definite so dense
it feels like drowning. Grant Wood
turned everything to cauliflower,

the rounded contours of a thunderhead,
flint-hard. He made us proud:
though all those edges might not be quite
the way it was, at least he'd tried.

"But it has no form!" they'd say to
the scribbler whose floundering fragments
kept getting out of hand—and who, either
fed up with or starved out of
her native sloughs, would, stowed aboard
the usual nomadic moving van, trundle her
dismantled sensibility elsewhere.

Europe, that hodgepodge of ancestral
calamities, was hard and handsome, its rubble
confident, not shriveling on the vine,
as here, like an infertile melon—the Virgin
jejune in her grotto of cold plaster, half sick
of that sidelong enclave, the whispered "Cathlick."

Antiquity unshrouds on wimpling canvas,
adjunct of schoolhouse make-believe: the Italy
of urns and cypresses, of stairways
evolving toward a state of mind
not to be found except backstage
among hunchbacks and the miscreants
who control the scenery, flanked
by a pair of masks whose look, at even
this remove, could drill through bone:
the tragic howl, the comic rictus,
eyeholes that stare out of the crypt

of what no grownup is ever heard to speak of
but in the strangled tone whose lexicon
is summed up in one word: *Bankrupt*.

Bankrupt: the abysm of history,
a slough to be pulled out of
any way you could. Antiquity, the backward
suction of the dark, amounted to a knothole
you plugged with straw, old rags, pages
ripped from last year's Sears Roebuck catalog,
anything, to ward off the blizzard.

Not so, for the born-again, the
shuddering orifices of summer.
On prayer-meeting night, outside
the vestibule among multiple
bell-pulls of Virginia creeper,
the terrible clepsydra of becoming
distils its drop: a luna moth, the emblem
of the born-again, furred like an orchid
behind the ferned antennae, a totem-
garden of lascivious pheromones,
hangs, its glimmering streamers
pierced by the dripstone burin of the eons
with the predatory stare out of the burrow,
those same eyeholes. Imago
of unfathomable evolvings, living
only to copulate and drop its litter,
does it know what it is, what it has been,
what it may or must become?

STACKING THE STRAW

In those days the oatfields'
fenced-in vats of running platinum,
the yellower alloy of wheat and barley,
whose end, however gorgeous all that trammeled
rippling in the wind, came down
to toaster-fodder, cereal
as a commodity, were a rebuke
to permanence—to bronze or any metal
less utilitarian than the barbed braids
that marked off a farmer's property,
or the stoked dinosaur of a steam engine
that made its rounds from farm to farm,
after the grain was cut and bundled,
and powered the machine that did the threshing.

Strawstacks' beveled loaves, a shape
that's now extinct, in those days were
the nearest thing the region had
to monumental sculpture. While hayracks
and wagons came and went, delivering bundles,
carting the winnowed ore off to the granary,

a lone man with a pitchfork stood aloft
beside the hot mouth of the blower,
building about himself, forkful
by delicately maneuvered forkful,
a kind of mountain, the golden
stuff of mulch, bedding for animals.
I always thought of him with awe—

a craftsman whose evolving altitude
gave him the aura of a hero. He'd come down
from the summit of the season's effort
black with the baser residues of that
discarded gold. Saint Thomas of Aquino
also came down from the summit
of a lifetime's effort, and declared
that everything he'd ever done was straw.

TEPOZTLÁN

The Aztecs, conquering, brought Huitzilopochtli
and ceremonial slitting the heart out; Cortés,
a.k.a. Son of the Sun, along with new weapons,
El Señor and the Virgin of the Remedies,
introduced heaven and hell (which the Tepoztecans
never quite took hold of); the gringos
arrived with sanitary arrangements
and a great many questions.
                              Autonomy
climbed down from the plane empty-handed,
carrying only introspection and a few
self-canceling tropisms, innocent
of history as any peasant, to travel,
all in a day, from upland maguey fields'
clumped pewter prongs through treetop regions
where songbirds bright as parrots flashed
uncaged, living free as fishes; alongside
churches of ice-cream-tinted stone
carved like a barbed music, and vendors
of a poisoned rainbow—*helados, refrescos,*
nopals, papayas, mangos, melons all swarming
with warned-against amoebas—down
through villages smelling of pulque,
jasmine and dysentery; past haciendas
torpid with dust, the dogs owned by nobody,
the burros, whether led or tethered, all
long-suffering rancor, the stacked coffins
waiting, mainly child-size (fatality,
part jaguar, part hummingbird, part

gila monster, alive and well here,
clearly needs children); through the daily
dust-laying late-afternoon rainstorm,
in cadenced indigenous place-names
the drip of a slow waterfall,
or of foliage when the rain stops—
arriving, just after sundown,
at the town of Tepoztlán.

                Autonomy,
unaware that in some quarters
the place was famous, saw hanging
cliffs dyed a terrible heart-color
in the gloaming light; a marketplace
empty of people; a big double-towered
church whose doors stood open. No one
inside but a sexton in white *calzoni*,
sweeping up a litter that appeared
to be mainly jasmine: so much fragrance,
so much death, such miracles—El Señor,
glitter-skirted, casketed upright in glass—
such silence . . . until, for no known reason,
overhead the towered bells broke out
into such a pounding that bats, shaken
from their hooked-accordion sleep
by the tumult, poured onto the dark,
a river of scorched harbingers
from an underworld the Tepoztecans
don't altogether believe in.

                They speak

on occasion of Los Aires, or, in their
musical Nahuatl, of *Huehuetzintzin,*
the Old Ones. Who knows what ultimately
is, and what's mere invention? Autonomy,
encapsuled and enmembraned hitherto
by a deaf anxiety, left Tepoztlán
marked, for the first time ever,
by the totally unlooked-for—by a
halfway belief that from out there,
astoundingly, there might be,
now and then, some message.

THE RESERVOIRS
OF MOUNT HELICON

The monks are dying out at Hosios Loukas.
At Great Vespers the celebrant,
singing alone in a cracked ancient voice
while I hug the stall, sole auditor,
keeps losing his place in the chant-book's
stiff curled parchment. Having come by taxi
all the way from Delphi (the driver waits
outside, in no hurry) to be mowed down by a tsunami
of Greek voices, I experience only
the onset of an urge to giggle.
                                    The mosaics
are hardly up to the postcards; tourists,
now that there's a highway, arrive
by the busload. But the ride up—
wet appletrees' cusp-studded wands
aped by the unlikely topside hue of crows
braking and turning just below eye level—
is worth it, and so are the plane trees
that grow here: huge as churches,
they might go back a thousand years, be older
than Hosios Loukas, whose hermitage this was,
be older even than Luke the painter
of seraphic epiphanies. He'd have found it
strange here: the light all muzzy silver,
Helicon green and vast across a mist-
hung gorge, these plane trees
so palpably, venerably pagan—
but I think he might have liked it.

Waiting

outside for the vesper bell, I fell into
conversation with a monk—one of fifteen
now remaining, he told me—who spoke a kind
of English learned, and since largely forgotten,
during a sojourn in Brooklyn. They'd been building
a bridge then, he recalled, across the Hudson;
he supposed it must be finished by now.
I told him, in a faint voice, yes,
it had been finished—and looked out, whelmed
into vertigo by gulfs spanned for a moment
by so mere a thread, across a gorge
already half-imaginary with distance
toward the improbable, the muse-haunted
reservoirs of Mount Helicon.

TRASIMENE

Tourmaline plashing in a noose of reeds,
Lake Trasimene is being slowly strangled
in ecology, no respecter of the Quattrocento.
How could that sheeted
opacity be looked at, after Arezzo,
except as the filtered tint,
wet lake-hue into fresco, Piero
della Francesca laid like rain
over sky, drapery, the roofs of houses?
How, after Perugia, after the Louvre
and the Uffizi, can the Umbria
of Perugino be seen, five centuries later,
except as he pre-empted it?—as space
looking inward, transparency set breathing
to commend an attitude: Madonna,
head drooping like a tulip, among donors.
Fashions in felicity play hide and seek
with decor; reigning apostolates
shrink to a simper. It's the lake's
look that breathes here,
infinity's eutrophic emerald
that won't keep either.

RAIN AT BELLAGIO

for Doris Thompson Myers

I

The omnipresence of the sound of water: rain
on the graveled walks, the lakeside terraces,
the red pantiles of Bellagio.

At Paestum we had not heard it.
An acreage of thyme, winnowed by sea breezes.
A line of blue out past the silted harbor—
unauthenticated because unheard,
a scene one might have dreamed.

At Herculaneum, a stoppage of the ears.
Cicadas mute, an oleander stillness.
Rancor of cypresses. Impacted fire.
Effete ribaldry strangling in hot mud
up to the nostrils. Water stricken
from the ledgers of memory.

At Naples, human noise inundating the bayfront,
lapping at castles' elephantine hooves, rampaging
tenement ravines. Once in the night
I woke and knew it had been raining—
not from the sound but from the smell, as though
an animal had left its spoor.

Under an aspect less clement, the trickle
of sewers, the vine-patched bombholes,

bambini with no underpants, gnarled women
wearing the black of perpetual resignation,
might have figured more gravely than as a condiment,
garlic for a week of living well.

2

Aboard the *wagons-lits* we drank Est! Est! Est!,
leaned tipsily out of windows, behaved
as though we owned the railway car, owned
the platform as it receded, owned even, overhead,
the diminution to a half-perceived scintilla
of the stars, after the manner of the young who travel
Europe, garnering experience in pairs.

We passed the Apennines asleep, and woke in a country
where the color of the olive trees was rainy.
Gray rain muddying the emerald of ricefields,
blurring, across the flood plain of the Po, the vague
geometry of poplars on the march—a part
of some interminable uprising.

At Milan a drizzle, the boulevards inlaid
with dun-colored patines, the slough of plane trees.
A car sent from the villa, behind whose steamed windows
we talk as freely as though the driver had no ears.
Glimpsing, through the sheets of rain, the first gray-green,

narrow windings of Lake Como,
the red pantiles of Monza and Lecco,
the little farms, the villa walls
sequestering unimagined pleasures. Vineyards.
Terraces. The starred darkness of lemon trees
through the downpour. Gravel under our shoes,
a footman holding an umbrella. All as in
that terrifying place where no one is admitted
whose taste is not impeccable.

3

Servants. The butler's practiced deference,
the liquid glance unerring as a falcon's—
a lisp in the shrubbery, a blur of wingbars
and he's placed you. On the hall table
tuberoses' opening racemes purport a sadness
the equal of Elysium. Massed carnations
in a cushioned bedroom, a bath overlooking
the flutter of chaffinches, cypresses'
columned melancholy, the lacquered foliage
of magnolias seen from the balcony, are no refuge
from the surveillance of chambermaids, scathing
as a penitent's examination of conscience.
The scuffed suitcase cannot escape: as soon as
your back is turned, they have
already unpacked it.

Out on the lake a white traghetto, moving
almost without pause from one shore to the other,
a punctual amphibious spider, skeins
into one zigzag the descending
clatter from the campaniles of Bellagio,
of Varenna and Cadenabbia, as though reining
the fragments of experience into one process—
being-and-becoming fused, a single scheme.

The rustle of descending silk (these shores
being mulberry country), the curtains drawn
against the prerogative of the chambermaids,
behind closed doors, having had our tea,
conspiratorially, two high-church Episcopalians, we begin
to read aloud the office of Compline.

The damask weave of luxury, the arras
of melodrama. A wailing about the eaves.
Confidences wading like a salvage operation
toward an untidy past: the admirer
who had in fact been a bricklayer,
who wore dirty undershirts; the rue
of not-yet-dealt-with gaffes, chagrins
and false positions, tinder
for the scorn of maître d's, the pained
look of a host whose taste is impeccable:
hazards of a murderous civility, the beast
snared in a nightmare of living well.

4

Cocktails in the salotto, underneath a portrait
of the late owner, a distiller's heiress
of dim but cultivated beauty, whose third spouse
left her title to an extinct principality. The villa,
acquired by caprice, became her favorite household.
Though in the way of moral character not much
is to be expected, *noblesse oblige*: the servants—
eighty of them altogether—must be provided for.
Emissaries of those foundations into which
the larger fortunes have unavoidably been siphoned
were circuitously whispered to; and so, the times
being what they have become, the princeliest
of the seventeen bedrooms, stripped
of its cushier urgings to dalliance,
is now a conference room—this week
for a conclave of jurisprudes, the week after
for experts in the field of public health
concerning the eradication of malaria.

Reclamation of the land: the labor gangs,
the overseers, the seasonal migrations,
the Lombard plain at last made habitable,
a source of fortunes: irrigated water meadows,
ricefields, wheat, mulberries, the channeled music
of the Po, the Oglio, the Adda, the Ticino. Vineyards.
Landed estates. Walled properties above Lake Como,
for the view. A rural proletariat whose fortunes
and miseries go unrecorded.

5

In her declining years the Principessa
was to be seen leaning, as she made her rounds
nuzzled in sable against the lake damp,
on the arm of her butler.

The indispensable tyranny of servants.
Gardeners, kitchen maids, woodcutters, grooms,
footmen. Private secretaries.
Confessors. Archbishops.
Above the fever trap of the Maremma
the ritual complicity: in castle towers
the secret stair, the cached aconite,
the hired assassin.

Fiefdoms. Latifundia. The wealth of nations.
The widening distance between rich and poor,
between one branch and another of the tree of misery.
A view of lakeside terraces
to sell one's soul for.

6

Among the company at dinner, Professor B.,
reputedly the best mind in Italy,
who speaks no English; also Professor d'E.,
who speaks it more exquisitely than any native—
slim, fair, elfin, author of a legal treatise

9

The pang of bells, through rain-filled dark,
at every hour. Half slumber,
feeble morning light. At seven, booted
and raincoated, we're plunging through the wet
to board the traghetto—the only passengers,
along with a truckload of Italian beer—for Cadenabbia
and early communion at the English church.

A port, a buoy, a rudder: hymnbook similes
capsize in the act of kneeling
and receiving the substance of such controversy,
cataclysms from the winepress of the glaciers,
whatever it is that knows itself only
in the sense of being carried,
all the bridges out, surrounded
by the rush of moving water—total
self-abandonment perceived as living well.

A rush for the landing, the water rushing alongside,
down gutters, over cobblestones. In one hour
the level of the lake has risen astoundingly.
Aboard the traghetto, a priest
wears a violet-lined biretta
and buckles on his shoes.

Seeing how the picturesque outlives its meaning.

no one (he says) has read.
      —Then I will read it.
      —Oh, but really it is very dull.
The weather in Italy, he says, is changing.
Now that charcoal is no longer burned
extensively, the forests have grown up again,
forests draw moisture—*Ecco!*

Flooding along the Po, the Adige, the Ticino.
Dykes giving way at Ferrara, inundations
at Rimini, the beetfields of Ravenna
already under water. On the flood plain,
the mosaics of Sant' Apollinare in Classe
ripple as though drowned—redemption
envisioned as a wall of water.

7

What does a place like this not offer?
Flawless cuisine, a first-rate cellar,
mountain footpaths laced with wild cyclamen
and maidenhair; topiary, sunken gardens,
wood nymphs and a dying slave in marble; even,
when nothing short of total solitude
will do, a hermitage.

My friend is twenty,
blond as Lucrezia Borgia, her inclinations

nurtured with care since childhood.
She speaks three languages and has had
six proposals. Since January
her existence has been an exercise
in living like a Principessa. Her father
still cannot fathom what has happened.
He points, appealing, to a letter
on the hall table, overhung
by the tuberoses' extravagant love-death,
addressed to an abbess.

To *try her vocation,* as it seems the phrase goes.
As a nun. In an enclosed community.
Why in the world . . . ?

One might have said by way of a response (but did not)
that living under vows, affianced to a higher poverty,
might likewise be an exercise in living well.

8

Her last evening amounts to an exercise in prevarication.
Where precisely she is going, and why, she has
given up explaining. Dinner is a banquet. Afterward,
half sozzled on red wine followed by champagne
followed by Strega, we're in raincoats,
climbing into a villa car with a pair
of half-fledged jurisprudes. A halt

somewhere along the way, the rain slackening
and closing in again like trees in a landscape,
to snitch grapes from a vineyard. We arrive
at the farewell party pretending we're bacchan

Antique U.S. jazz on a portable phonograph.
Liqueurs. Chocolates. My friend dancing
the cha-cha-cha, engaging in mock flirtations
with a moody Italian, then with a cheerful one
whose profession entails the proliferation of sup
    —But how *can* you?
    —And why isn't what's good for your cou
      good also for Italy?

A prolonged huddle with the cheerful one. Eme
they announce they have an announcement:
they have decided to get married
for about a week. At midnight,
trying for a departure, we find the door
locked against us, the key hidden prettily
in somebody's décolletage. Everybody
is going away tomorrow. We say goodbye
to the jurisprudes, the young footman
standing expressionless beside the door.

10

Punctually at three in the afternoon, our luggage
waits by the door, the car stands in the rain,
its motor running. Bathos of tuberoses
on the hall table, the butler's formal bow,
the footman holding an umbrella. Gravel
under our shoes. Behind the steamed windows
confidences interspersed with silences.
At Milan, dim through fatigue, a watershed:
for the rest of our lives, we will be traveling
in opposite directions. Behind us, limestone
and chestnut mountainsides, streaming, release
their increment of moisture: rain, glacier melt,
the wine of change. Ahead of us,
spilling across the lap of Italy, the tributaries
of the Po—the Adda, the Oglio, the Sesia—
mingle and descend toward Ferrara,
toward Rimini and Ravenna: uncontrollable
as rumor, as armies set in motion,
the sound of water.

11

Sometimes since, in dreams I find myself obliged
to assume, without previous instruction, control
of a plane I have no memory of boarding. I wake
without ever having learned the outcome. Or,

in another region, I find myself
face to face with the transparent strata
of experience, the increment of years,
as a wall of inundation, the drowned mosaic
glimmering above the flood plain. Waking,
I hear the night sounds merge, a single rustle
as of silk, as though becoming might amend,
unbroken, to one stilled, enclosing skein.

12

At the Abbey, between the shored-up Norman church
and the trefoiled oak of the pilgrim hostel,
running liquid and garrulous through a life of silence,
cushioned and tended between banks of tamed wildflowers,
the sound of water: indivisible, unstilled,
unportioned by the bells that strike the hours.